MW01119978

# Direct Marketing
## in a week

### DEE TWOMEY

## Hodder & Stoughton

A MEMBER OF THE HODDER HEADLINE GROUP

*To my three fine sons Louis, George and Joe*

Thanks to Sighle, my mum, for her extraordinary kindness.
Special thanks to Mark, ever the voice of reason.

Thanks also to the many professional enthusiasts who have
shared their wisdom along the way. It's been fun.

Orders: please contact Bookpoint Ltd, 130 Milton Park, Abingdon, Oxon
OX14 4SB.
Telephone: (44) 01235 827720, Fax: (44) 01235 400454. Lines are open from
9.00–6.00, Monday to Saturday, with a 24 hour message answering service.
Email address: orders@bookpoint.co.uk

*British Library Cataloguing in Publication Data*
A catalogue record for this title is available from The British Library

ISBN 0 340 85765x

First published 2003
Impression number   10 9 8 7 6 5 4 3 2 1
Year                2007 2006 2005 2004 2003

Copyright © 2003 Dee Twomey

Cover image: Photodisc/ Getty Images

Typeset by SX Composing DTP, Rayleigh, Essex.
Printed in Great Britain for Hodder & Stoughton Educational, a division of
Hodder Headline Plc, 338 Euston Road, London NW1 3BH by
Cox & Wyman Ltd, Reading, Berkshire.

## The leading organisation for professional management

As the champion of management, the Chartered Management Institute shapes and supports the managers of tomorrow. By sharing intelligent insights and setting standards in management development, the Institute helps to deliver results in a dynamic world.

## Setting and raising standards

The Institute is a nationally accredited organisation, responsible for setting standards in management and recognising excellence through the award of professional qualifications.

## Encouraging development, improving performance

The Institute has a vast range of development programmes, qualifications, information resources and career guidance to help managers and their organisations meet new challenges in a fast-changing environment.

## Shaping opinion

With in-depth research and regular policy surveys of its 91,000 individual members and 520 corporate members, the Chartered Management Institute has a deep understanding of the key issues. Its view is informed, intelligent and respected.

For more information call 01536 204222 or visit www.managers.org.uk

# C O N T E N T S

Direct marketing has seen a sustained and dramatic rise in importance. Over the last year alone, expenditure grew by 10 per cent on all forms of direct marketing. You would be hard pressed to find an organisation or industry that is not using direct marketing to help achieve its aims. This sector is now worth over £11 billion, according to the Direct Marketing Association (census 2001/02). Skilled direct marketers are very much in demand.

The term direct marketing is a convenient shorthand for the process of recording information about an individual's responses to plan, target and implement marketing activity, in order to win and keep customers.

Computing power has allowed direct marketing to evolve. Instead of running blanket advertising campaigns designed for the typical customer, you can now develop a dialogue with a real individual and track what happens over time.

Technology continues to move direct marketing forward. Call centre spend now exceeds spend on direct mail and internet integration has become a vital consideration.

Add direct marketing skills to your portfolio and become a key player in the business of acquiring, developing and retaining customers.

Your journey to direct marketing success will take you through seven crucial steps, from taking stock of your current situation through to measuring the results of your carefully managed plans and campaigns.

# Customers, competitors and capability

Prepare yourself for a stimulating week, tackling the concepts and practicalities of direct marketing. Today you will take stock of your customers, competitors and your own organisation's direct marketing capability. This forms a solid knowledge base upon which you can develop your strategies and campaigns.

## What is direct marketing?

Ask ten different marketing practitioners and you will get ten different answers to this question, for instance:

- 'It's the same thing as database marketing.'
- 'It's like ordinary marketing only it's direct to the customer whether by post, over the phone or on the net.'
- 'It's a sales channel instead of a traditional sales force.'
- 'Call it response marketing and you've summed it up.'

These statements contain some truth, but they are misleading because they do not tell the whole truth. The overriding trademark of direct marketing compared to traditional marketing is that it uses information about customers and prospects at an individual level.

The distinguishing features of direct marketing are:

- Customer's insights are based upon individual data
- All communication is designed to get a response
- Marketing databases facilitate interaction and personalisation
- Every aspect of a direct marketing campaign can be tested
- Results can be accurately measured
- Strategies are based on both customer acquisition and, importantly, on customer retention.

Acquiring a new customer can cost ten times more than keeping an existing customer. Therefore, it makes financial sense to encourage loyalty.

Whether your target customers are consumers or businesses, direct marketing works in the same way.

LOYALTY LADDER

ADVOCATE

CUSTOMER

PROSPECT

SUSPECT

A wide variety of marketing activity is considered to be direct marketing if it involves a response mechanism, including direct mail, telemarketing, TV and press advertising, web banner ads, door drops and inserts.

Take direct mail as an example and you can see the importance of direct marketing. The Direct Mail Information Service reports that expenditure on direct mail has increased by 150 per cent over the last ten years. Within this time, volumes have doubled with over 4.9 million items mailed in the year 2001, with a split of 75 per cent consumer and 25 per cent business. This activity is worth £2,228 million in the UK alone. It is big and it is growing.

## Taking stock of customers, competitors and capability

Before you start planning, build up your knowledge of:

- *Your customers*: everything you do depends on understanding customers. To develop an effective strategy you must know who your customers are now and who they might be in the future.
- *Your capability*: you need to be sure of what you can and cannot achieve. An audit of your current direct marketing capability is essential.
- *Your competitors*: your customers are not just influenced by your company. They make choices by comparing your company with its competitors. You need to provide a compelling reason for customers to choose you and to stay loyal.

## Get to know your customers

Recent research shows that only half of businesses have the ability to analyse the value of individual customers. Around ten per cent of businesses do not know precisely how many customers they have. Many cannot identify why they lose customers or which customers they are most likely to lose next.

To win in direct marketing, having a good understanding of your customers will put you ahead of the pack.

## The right customers

Consider that not all customers are equal. Some will help you and others will hinder you. Like good friends, you should choose your customers carefully.

| Good customers | Bad customers |
|---|---|
| High value | Low value |
| Cross-range buyers | Single purchase |
| Open to offers | Responders who never buy |
| Easy to maintain | Persistent complainers |
| Brand respecters | Fraudsters |
| Repeat buyers | High-risk customers |
| Positive opinion leaders | Negative opinion leaders |
| Loyal | Switchers |

Of course the definition of good and bad customers depends on your market. Try to create a definition of your good and bad customers.

## Customer knowledge

Answer these ten critical questions to gain insights into the profile and behaviour of your customers.

| | |
|---|---|
| 1. Who are your customers? | 6. What do they want? |
| 2. What do they buy? | 7. Are they satisfied? |
| 3. When do they buy? | 8. Are they promotionally responsive? |
| 4. How do they buy? | 9. Are they likely to switch? |
| 5. Why do they buy? | 10. What are they worth? |

## What are they worth?

One of the key differences between a good and bad customer is the value they represent to your organisation. There are various ways to assess customer value. The most popular are:

- Pareto 80:20 analysis
- Recency, frequency, monetary value
- Lifetime value

*Pareto 80:20*

You may be familiar with Pareto's 80:20 rule. Applied to business the rule states that 80 per cent of sales are generated by 20 per cent of customers.

The Pareto principle is enlightening. While the ratio may vary for different businesses, the principle is the same. This should alert you to the fact that a few customers are holding your whole organisation together.

Here are some examples for the consumer goods market:

| | | |
|---|---|---|
| Spreadable margarine | 5% customers | 65% sales |
| Canned beer | 15% adults | 90% sales |
| Washing powder | 35% customers | 65% sales |

By undertaking a Pareto analysis of customers, you have taken an important step towards knowing which customers to target. Recency, frequency and monetary value (RFM) calculations and customer lifetime value (LTV) provide further insights.

*Recency, frequency and monetary value*
The RFM model uses information about past buying behaviour to draw conclusions about customer value. This model was largely developed to assess the relative value of customers buying from catalogues. Key questions are:

- How long ago did they buy?
- How often do they buy?
- How much do they spend?

Look at two book club customers:

| RFM attribute | Mr Eve | Ms Adam |
|---|---|---|
| Recency | Six months ago | This month |
| Frequency | Every three months | Monthly |
| Monetary value | £25 | £10 |

In one year Ms Adam spends £120, while Mr Eve only spends £50, despite having a higher order value.

A combination of recency, frequency and monetary value can be used to create a score for each customer, based upon their past behaviour. The score you develop should reflect the relative value of customers to your particular business. As a general guide, frequency has the greatest impact on customer value as follows:

| Factor | Weighting |
|---|---|
| Recency | Multiply by 2 |
| Frequency | Multiply by 3 |
| Monetary value | Multiply by 1 |

*Lifetime value*

The lifetime value (LTV) model is used to calculate the total worth of a customer for the duration of that time they are your customer.

Using LTV is helpful because:

- A customer is worth much more than their initial purchase or Year 1 value
- Customer acquisition costs can be offset against future revenues
- Likely retention rates must be forecast
- It encourages strategic planning
- Every organisation must consider what a 'lifetime' means to them – do customers stay for 25 years or three months?
- Future conditions may change, so assumptions can be made clear and varied to test financial sensitivity

*Simple LTV formula*

LTV can be calculated by:

| Average spend (or profit) per purchase | × | Number of purchases per customer lifetime | = LTV. |

*Complex LTV formula*

LTV is a forecast of future revenue and thus the value of such 'future' revenue should be discounted back to today's prices. This creates what the accountants call Net Present Value (NPV).

| Lifetime value model | | | |
|---|---|---|---|
| | Year 1 | Year 2 | Year 3 |
| A  Number of new customers | 1000 | 500 | 275 |
| B  Retention rate (% kept into next year) | 50% | 55% | 60% |
| C  Sales per annum per customer | £600 | £600 | £600 |
| D  Total sales (A × C) | £600,000 | £300,000 | £165,000 |
| **Contribution** | | | |
| E  Net profit @ 20% (D × 20%) | £120,000 | £60,000 | £33,000 |
| **Discounted contribution** | | | |
| F  Discount rate @ 10% p.a. | 1 | 1.10 | 1.21 |
| G  NPV contribution (E × F) | £120,000 | £54,545 | £27,273 |
| H  Cumulative NPV contribution | £120,000 | £174,545 | £201,818 |
| I  Lifetime value @ NPV for each new customer (H ÷ A in Year 1) | £120 | £174.55 | £201.82 |

In this example, 1,000 new customers provide a lifetime value of £201 profit each within 3 years.

Use Pareto, RFM and LTV models to help you decide which customers are right for your business.

## Understanding your company's capability

With a clear focus on the right customers, you can really make an impact. However, you need to understand your company's current capability. Get a clear view by answering these ten vital questions. Ask your planners, sales force, agencies, call centre and marketing team. But remember to qualify anecdotal evidence with hard facts.

---

1. What market position does your company hold?
2. How does your brand and product compare to the opposition?
3. How many stages are there in the sales process?
4. What media do you use and why?
5. What marketing database capability exists?
6. How is direct marketing structured and resourced?
7. Is direct marketing represented at Board level?
8. What budget is available?
9. How do plans get approved?
10. What direct marketing expertise is available?

---

The better you know your current set up, the better placed you are to capitalise upon it and improve it. If a radical overhaul is not possible, be realistic about what you can achieve. The beauty of direct marketing is that you can introduce improvements over time.

## Tuning in to your competitors

It is unusual to have no direct competitors. In fact, your customer may also be your competitor's customer at another time or for another product or service. Where customers can choose between several suppliers, what share of customer spend does your company have on that category of goods? If you had to answer the ten critical customer questions for your competitors' customers, how would your answers differ?

Think about how your market will change in future. Which products, regions, services, sectors and channels are going to become more important? Will there be more competition or less? Greater demand or a shrinking market? Where possible, develop predictions about how your competitors may behave in future and how this will impact upon your own situation.

You can access a wealth of information from the professional institutes, via the internet, from public libraries and from your market research department. Companies like Thomson Intermedia and Neilsen Media Research provide a monitoring service covering competitors' TV, press, internet, direct mail and door drop activity.

Remember that your direct marketing activity does not happen in a vacuum. Consider how your competitors do their marketing. To be heard above the noise, you need to be clear about what you have to offer and be clever about how you construct your campaigns.

It is far easier to be successful if you can offer something different and better than the competition. The difference may be:

- Brand image
- Technical superiority
- Innovation
- Value for money
- Quality of product
- Consistency of service delivery
- Geographic coverage
- Speed of delivery
- Customer service

If there is truly no difference between what you can offer to customers and what your competitors offer, then why should anyone choose you? Identify your company's distinctive competence before you begin to develop your direct marketing strategy. Then the fun can really begin.

## Summary

Today you have learnt about the essential features of direct marketing. Direct marketing focuses on marketing to individual customers and prospects. Pareto, RFM and LTV models allow you to identify the right customers to target.

Remember that customer retention is a key strategic goal over and above customer acquisition. This is due to the commercial value of keeping the customers that you have won.

Having reached conclusions about your customers, competitors and direct marketing capability, you are now in a good position to tackle strategic planning and objective setting.

# Planning your strategy and setting objectives

Today you will learn how to develop a direct marketing plan by identifying issues, setting objectives and deciding on strategy. Planning is a crucial stage of direct marketing. It requires clear thinking and creativity to come up with the right approach.

## The importance of planning

There is an old business saying: 'People don't plan to fail, they fail to plan.'

These warning signs indicate poor planning:

- Lack of clarity about the targets to be achieved
- Inappropriate strategies for the market or organisation
- Confused messages and policies
- Unachievable time-scales and unclear responsibilities

Good planning is apparent when:

- Everyone is clear about their role and company mission
- The strategy fits the situation
- Every element of the campaign supports the overall message
- The action plan is realistic with clear interim deadlines

## Situational analysis

Start with a situational analysis. It allows you to consolidate the information you have on your own capability, customers, competitors and the market place. This entails defining your organisation aims, compiling a SWOT analysis and identifying issues.

## Organisation aims

Start by writing down the broad aims or mission of your organisation. This may be very easy or very difficult, depending upon the volatility of your market and the clarity of your company's mission. Here are some examples of organisation aims:

- To be the leading online banking company
- To provide the highest quality business travel experience
- To be amongst the top three electronic component manufacturers

Once you have clarified why your company exists and whom it serves, you can perform a SWOT analysis.

## SWOT up

Organise the information you have gathered about your customers, capability and competitors into a SWOT analysis. SWOT simply stands for:

- Strengths
- Weaknesses
- Opportunities
- Threats

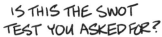

Strengths and weaknesses are internal to your company and opportunities and threats are external. An example of a SWOT for a mobile telecoms company might be:

| **Strengths** | **Weaknesses** |
|---|---|
| Large consumer base | Low business customer base |
| High brand awareness | Customer attrition |
| Extensive distribution | Inflexible customer database |
| Technological innovation | Speed of product development |
| **Opportunities** | **Threats** |
| Penetrate business market | Saturation of market |
| Attract high profit customers | Share price volatility |
| New technological possibilities | Regulatory restrictions |
| Reduce customer defections | Environmental pressure groups |

## Identify the real issues

From the SWOT analysis, decide which things are the fundamental issues and challenges.

For the mobile telecoms company, issues might include:

- The need for detailed research and database analysis to gain understanding of customers
- Improvement in speed of product development and launch
- The need to increase customer loyalty

Take care to make the issues as precise as possible. Use available research, management information and the customer database to prioritise the key issues. By understanding where you are now, you can plan for where you want to be tomorrow.

## Destination, direction and delivery

Let's turn to the main elements of the planning process.

| Destination | Objective | Where do you want to get to? |
|---|---|---|
| Direction | Strategy | How will you get there? |
| Delivery | Plan | What steps will you take to get there? |

Your objective is the destination you want to reach. The strategy you select is the one that you feel gives you the best chance of getting there. Detailed action plans are then required to deliver the strategy.

## Setting objectives

The higher you go within an organisation, the more you will be called upon to set objectives and strategy, and the less time you will have to handle implementation of plans. The most common types of corporate goals are:

- To grow market share
- To increase sales
- To improve profits
- To reduce costs

Within these company goals, the role direct marketing plays will vary and can result in these broad objectives:

- To find new customers
- To retain customers for longer
- To attract non-users and/or competitors' customers
- To increase the frequency of purchase
- To increase average order values
- To introduce differential pricing
- To reduce costs of acquiring and servicing customers
- To generate incremental sales from existing customers
- To introduce or exploit certain distribution channels

## Golden rules for setting objectives

Unless you are specific about your destination, how will you know when you have got there? Set precise objectives. Check them against the SMART criteria:

| S | Specific |
|---|----------|
| M | Measurable |
| A | Accurate and aspirational |
| R | Realistic |
| T | Time-bound |

Here are a couple of SMART objectives:

- We will increase online sales from our core sports catalogue from £700 to £780 million by year end
- We will increase our business customer base from 4000 to 6000 by 2010

Your objective represents your destination. Now that you know where you are going, how will you get there?

## Strategic direction

Consider the marketplace and your organisation's position within it. Decide how you will compete for business.

There are many strategic choices to be made, starting with deciding which markets (or market segments) to compete in and then how to compete.

## Which markets? What profit?

Choose which markets (or segments within a market) to compete in by assessing the opportunity they represent. Consider the impact of alternatives by using the PROFIT model:

**P**   Potential – market size and growth

**R**   Risk – degree of risk and chance of success

**O**   Obstructions – market accessibility and barriers to entry

**F**   Fit – appropriateness and fit with your business

**I**   Investment – scale of investment required

**T**   Turnover – revenue and profit available

Your choices can be summarised by looking at which markets you will compete in and with which products.

| | | Products | |
|---|---|---|---|
| | | Existing | New |
| **Markets** | Existing | Market penetration | Product development |
| | New | Market extension | Diversification |

## Strategic choices

Work through the strategic dimensions listed here to decide upon your direct marketing strategy.

- Existing or new markets
- Acquire new customers or retain existing customers
- Retain, develop, replace or create entirely new brand
- Target customers or prospects and current segments, select segments or new segments
- Convert competitors' customers or attract non-users
- Increase order value (up-sell) or increase customer value (cross-sell)
- Build the customer database or maintain and utilise it
- Refine media focus or expand media coverage
- Communicate with customers more often or less often

- Distribute exclusively directly to the customer or via wholesale, retail, agents, company salesperson or dovetail with these channels
- Position competitive offering based on quality, price, speed, size, reach, accessibility, service, range or image
- Promote existing product, develop, extend range, replace or update
- Price as high or low cost, select terms and payment methods
- Innovate to be a trailblazer or competent follower
- Sell via a one-stage or two-stage process (i.e. order now versus send for information)
- Attract responses in person, by internet, phone or coupon
- Promote via telemarketing, direct mail, TV, press, inserts, door drops, web banner ads and links or e-mail

Having read this list you will realise that these are not all absolute choices between one approach and another. It is possible, even desirable, to adopt a strategy of retaining existing customers while planning to acquire new customers.

Even the most successful business, with a high degree of customer loyalty, will experience a natural attrition. This happens as existing consumers move, change their lifestyle or pass away and as business customers move, merge, rationalise or cease trading.

## Strategic difference

Compared to other facets of marketing, direct marketing strategy usually encompasses:

- Market segmentation
- Customer acquisition strategy
- Customer retention strategy
- Database building and utilisation
- Targeted media selection
- Testing

Make certain that your strategy includes these important aspects.

Be sure that every issue you have identified in the situational analysis is addressed through your strategy. Involve key players in the process and stimulate fresh thinking and creative solutions.

## Turning dreams into reality

Once you have decided on your strategic approach, you must develop a campaign plan to bring your strategy to life. We will explain targeting, databases, media and campaign planning in the next chapters. At this stage, you need to know that a campaign plan clearly lays out what must be done, when and by whom. The plan is the mechanism through which you can deliver your strategy and achieve your direct marketing goals.

## Writing your direct marketing strategy

To gain agreement to your strategic approach, write a succinct report. Within it, explain why you recommend this particular direction, how it will work, what it will cost and what the payback will be. The format of this report should include the following sections.

*An overview*
• *Executive summary*: one-page précis of objectives, issues, strategy, budget and financial justification.

*Background*
• *Terms of reference*: who has commissioned the report, its purpose, sources of information and background.
• *Situational analysis*: brief review of the market, company, capability, customers and competitors.
• *Learnings from past campaigns*: conclusions from past activity based on analysis of facts, not hearsay.
• *Issues*: the major obstacles facing the business.

*Objectives, recommended strategy and campaigns*
- *Objectives*: SMART aims, often expressed as profit or sales revenue, numbers of new customers, registrations on to loyalty schemes or websites, often covering a three-year period.
- *Strategic recommendation*: the overall strategic approach to be adopted, together with the budget requirement, covering the chosen market, acquisition and retention, research and analysis, database and media.
- *Operational campaign plan*: detailed action plans for Year 1 and outline actions for Years 2–3, showing how the strategy will be implemented, including responsibilities, deadlines and interim targets.

*Contingencies, financials and assumptions*
- *Contingencies*: anticipated action if you do not meet or exceed plan targets, if market conditions change, if regulations change, if competitors take certain actions.
- *Budget*: the budget required to implement the campaign, broken down by activity type.
- *Financial justification*: showing the cost-benefit of the strategy. Typically including a return on investment (ROI) and lifetime value analysis.
- *Assumptions*: setting out the judgements that have been made to develop the plan, e.g. interest rates, attrition rates, response rates.

*Detailed analysis, schedules and projections*
- *Appendices*: includes all the detailed analysis to support the conclusions of the strategy, campaign time-scales, media schedules and detailed response and conversion projections.

## Summary

Today you have found out about setting objectives and developing a direct marketing strategy. Remember to:

- Develop your plans based on an understanding of your company's aims and situation
- Complete a SWOT analysis and identify the key issues
- Get SMART by setting objectives which are specific, measurable, accurate and aspirational, realistic and time-bound
- Select the strategic direction that can deliver your company to its chosen destination
- Ensure that your strategy includes research and analysis, acquisition, retention, database development, segmentation and targeted media
- Bring your strategy to life with an operational campaign plan
- Put your strategy in writing to gain agreement and get the go-ahead from your organisation

Time spent planning is rarely wasted. It means you are well placed to develop alternatives if problems arise. It also means that you can exploit opportunities as they arise. Preparation is the direct marketer's friend.

# Finding and keeping the right customers

You now know how to assess customer value through techniques such as Pareto 80:20, lifetime value and recency frequency and monetary value analysis. Yet how do you find and keep the right customers? Segmentation and targeting provide the solution.

## How does segmentation help?

Direct marketing is all about communicating with individuals on a personal basis. However, how can you make sense of large volumes of data to target customers and potential customers? Segmentation allows you to divide up your market into customer groups or segments. Customers within a segment are similar to each other and dissimilar to other groups of customers in other segments.

Segmentation then, is used to understand individual customers in the market place and to group them together to form distinct segments which are identifiable, accessible and substantial.

At its simplest, a consumer segmentation may be:

- Non-user
- Competitor's customer
- Low-value customer
- High-value customer

For business markets, simple segmentation may be:

- Small company
- Medium company
- Large company

In business markets, segmentation is often used to make selling more cost effective by prioritising the companies that require regular face-to-face salespeople and that can be served better by telesales and direct distribution.

## How to segment

Market segmentation involves finding out the key drivers that distinguish one group of customers from another.

The key drivers of consumer market segmentation tend to be:

1 Geo-demographic – who they are: age, gender, class, location
2 Lifestyle – how they live: income, occupation,

family/household composition, interests
3 Attitudinal – why they buy: motivation to select your product, e.g. price, image, application, benefit
4 Transactional – what, how and how much they buy

The key drivers of business segmentation are:

1 Company size – by turnover, employees, growth
2 Industry sector – nature of business, market place
3 Company location – geographic location and environment
4 Purchases and people – products bought, value and method of purchase, buying policy and role in decision-making process

Statistical modelling techniques can be used to isolate the key drivers and to identify customer clusters or groups. Alternatively, you can use off-the-shelf segmentation classification systems.

## Off-the-peg segmentation systems

Ready-made segmentation systems can be extremely useful where you have limited data on your prospects and customers.

Geo-demographic consumer systems use individual Census data such as age and home ownership, to classify postcodes into neighbourhood types. The resulting segments are self-explanatory: for example: well off, white-collar families with older children. By providing a customer list with postcodes, you can classify which segment your customers belong to. Consumer segmentation products include:

- Acorn from CACI, UK geo-demographic founder
- Cameo from EuroDirect
- Mosaic from Experian
- Prizm and Psycl£ from Claritas

Specialist products also exist: for instance, Scottish Acorn, Financial Mosaic and Cameo Property.

Basic business segmentation can be achieved using information about limited and public companies, made available through Companies House classifications:

- Standard Industry Code (SIC) classification by industry sector
- Size of company

Segmentation, whether bespoke or off the shelf, helps to make sense of customers and prospects in the marketplace. It allows you to decide which segments to target within your campaigns.

## What is targeting?

Forget the need for a bow and arrow, with 'targeting' you aim for the target by reaching the right customers, in the right place, with the right message and at the right time.

Targeting is the process of identifying and reaching specific individuals in order to attract and retain them as customers. All targeting is designed to elicit a response in the most cost-effective manner.

## The importance of targeting

When developing a direct marketing campaign, in addition to the product or service by segment, you need to consider:

1 Targeting
2 Offer
3 Timing
4 Creative (design and copywriting treatment)
5 Response mechanism

These factors are ranked in priority order, following the test results of an extensive consumer campaign (study by Ogilvy and Mather), and experience of other campaigns supports this ranking. A change of creative or response device can create a small improvement in results. Targeting, however, can account for an improvement of six times the response, comparing the best to worst performing list of names and addresses.

Remember this if your senior manager critiques your next planned campaign. It is human nature for creative concepts to spark off opinions from just about everyone. Nevertheless, while creative treatments are important, targeting has the greatest impact on results.

## Who will you target?

Create a target profile that describes who you are targeting. Consider the following targeting dimensions for consumers and businesses.

*Consumer*

- Which segment?
- Status – prospect or customer
- Value – high, medium or low value
- Products and services used
- Geodemographic profile – age, gender, location
- Lifestage – e.g. young family, retired
- Attitudes – e.g. brand loyal or not
- Lifestyle – e.g. struggling to survive or wealthy professional

*Business-to-business*
Many of the consumer dimensions still apply. Also consider:

- Role – decision maker, influencer, gatekeeper
- Past contact – none, responded, had appointment
- Company type – plc, ltd, partnership, sole trader
- Sector – industry sector
- Location type – high street, industrial park or campus

## Golden rules of targeting

- Ensure your targeting supports your strategy
- Describe your target profile as fully as possible, highlighting the most important customer attributes
- Specify who you do not want to attract, as well as who you do
- Create a targeting shorthand so that it can be understood, e.g. committed online purchasers
- Get scientific – use all the research and database analysis at your disposal
- Assess your choices of media, offer, timing, format and creative through your prospects' eyes
- Do not pay twice to reach the same people – eliminate potential duplicates
- Establish benchmark performance levels or controls and monitor results against these controls

## Types of targeting

Direct marketing is all about communicating with individuals. All media carries a call to action in order to encourage target customers to respond. Then we can gather individual data and make a sale. There are two types of targeting:

1  *Personalised targeting*: where you have individual's name and address records either on your database or from a bought-in list. For targeting using individual data, typical media are direct mail, telemarketing, e-mail and mobile short message service (SMS) text messaging.
2  *Broad-scale targeting*: where you do not have individual data – yet. When targeting without individual data, typical media are TV, press, door drops, internet banner ads and hyperlinks, directory listings and in-store point of sale.

## Personalised targeting

With a prospect and customer database, you can select the individuals you want to target with personalised communications. You can also make selections from external lists for prospecting purposes. Profiling and cloning techniques can help you to target more precisely.

*Database selections*

Accurate database targeting relies on the ability to select the
target customer group that you have defined. This means
that the data you hold for individuals must reflect the criteria
for your target.

Take the example of a direct music business. It has a new
boxed jazz collection available on CD. It wants to target high
spending customers who love jazz. To be able to do so their
database must record:

- Which individuals have bought (as opposed to
  simply enquired)
- Whether the CDs they have bought include jazz (all
  CD titles must be categorised by type of music)
- What they have spent by type of music and in total
  (sales over time must be grouped by customer, not
  simply recorded per mailshot or per product)

*Exclude the bad, mad and sad*

When defining the selections, make sure you state the
exclusions you want.

Potential exclusions:

- Opt outs – consumers asking not to be contacted,
  i.e. 'Do not mail me' and 'Unsubscribe' responses
- Unacceptable credit scores
- Incomplete name and address
- Gone aways – where mail and e-mail is undeliverable
- Mail, fax, phone or e-mail preference service
  suppressions (separate list of people who do not
  want to be contacted for marketing purposes)

- Deceased – bereavement register and mortality suppressions (compiled from the Register of Births and Deaths)
- Postcodes outside of the catchment area

The exact exclusions will depend on the nature of your business and the campaign.

*Using lists for targeting*
When you need to find new customers, you can make use of consumer and business lists. Data including name, address, phone number, fax and e-mail can be obtained, normally on a rental basis. There are many types of lists:

- Consumer lifestyle lists, such as Consodata and Experian
- Magazine subscriber lists
- Business lists
- Catalogue customers
- Event attendees lists

Selection criteria can be set in exactly the same way as your own database.

*Profiling and cloning*
Profiling is the process of identifying the discriminating characteristics of your customers. For example, a financial services company selling home insurance can carry out statistical modelling work to compare the characteristics of customers and unconverted enquirers. It may find that uptake improves if the person is aged 30–50, owns their own home and lives in leafy suburbs.

The company can use this information to improve its targeting and performance by:

- Identifying unconverted enquirers matching the profile and offering further incentives to buy
- Amending the media schedule to advertise in press titles which target the right audience
- Making selections from external lists

*Profiling service*
Many lifestyle list suppliers provide a valuable profiling service. Supply them with your campaign data, showing respondents and customers. They will be able to identify the discriminating characteristics between customers and non-buyers. They can also identify prospects that have the same characteristics as your customers – targeting lookalike individuals is known as cloning.

## Broad-scale targeting

You might wonder why you would ever do anything other than personalised communications within your direct marketing plan. After all, direct marketing is all about individual data, so why use broad-scale media at all? There are certain situations where broad-scale targeting is appropriate. For example where:

- There is no database yet, for instance, with a new business venture
- There are no repeat purchases and new customers are hard to identify, e.g. wedding services

- Your product or service has a mass audience, thus non-personalised media is the most cost-effective route, e.g. for utilities
- There is no other way to identify your target audience and you require prospects to take part in a hand-raising exercise, e.g. insurance claims assessors finding people who have had a recent accident

Select the media that provides sufficient coverage of your target audience for the least cost, based on your target profile. You can test the uplift created by integrating media.

Once you have decided on which media to use, maximise your targeting within each media.

**TV** Choose the right service, channels, days and programmes

**Radio** Select the most appropriate stations, timing, programmes and format

**Newspapers** Choose the papers, regional editions, pages, formats and positions that are appropriate, on the right days with the right offer

**Magazines** Advertise in the appropriate edition, with the right features at the right time

**Inserts** Target as for papers and magazines, but you will have more flexibility to target specific geographic regions

**Door drops** Identify the postcodes with a high percentage of households that match your target profile

**Internet banner ads and hyperlinks** Identify the suitable online communities, websites and portals, with the right content and advertise at the right time

**Directory listings and adverts** Select the crucial

directories and advertise in relevant regional or business versions, both hard copy and online or CD format

**In-store point of sale** Choose the right stores, shoppers, timing, location and make the right offer

**On-pack offers** Appeal to loyal or potential customers by using the right pack variants with the right offers

The offer, timing, format and creative treatment must all have a strong appeal to the people you want to attract. An example of good broad-scale targeting is promotion of kids' holiday clubs, targeted at parents via inserts in school newsletters and sent out just before the school holidays.

Broad-scale targeting generates responses from individual enquirers and customers which can be used for future, personalised targeting.

## Summary

- Segmentation allows you to simplify complex customer and marketplace information and to develop strategies and plans. Segments must be identifiable, accessible and substantial. You can build your own or use off-the-shelf segmentation systems.
- Profiling allows you to identify the distinguishing attributes of your customers. Cloning is the identification of prospects that match that profile.
- Precise targeting is vital for the success of your direct marketing activity. Having no individual data is not an excuse; even with broadscale media you can employ targeting techniques.
- When developing target profiles, it is crucial to ensure that your targeting supports your strategy and that you are clear which customers you need to avoid as well as attract.

# Building and using your marketing database

Direct marketing is often referred to as database marketing because of the pivotal role that the database plays in directing and controlling personal communications. Direct marketing strategy is incomplete if it does not provide direction on how the marketing database is to be built and used to achieve the organisation's aims. Understanding your customers, segmentation and targeting are all possible with the marketing database.

## What is a marketing database?

A marketing database is the engine that drives direct marketing forward. It is a set of computer files where data about individuals can be stored, accessed, analysed and retrieved to support direct marketing communications, which are designed to acquire and retain customers.

## Use your database strategically

- Assess market penetration and your customer profile compared to the market generally
- Understand the relative value of your customers
- Segment your customers and prospects into distinct groups
- Build a detailed profile of customers by segment
- Analyse the relative success of different campaigns

- Test new initiatives and assess likely take-up
- Forecast future sales, profit and return on investment

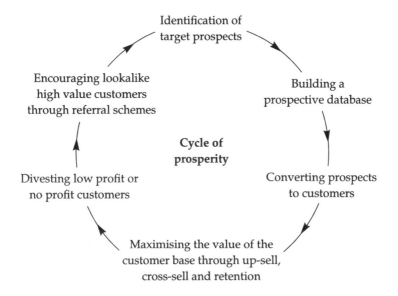

## Use your database operationally

- Select target customers and prospects for campaigns
- Manage magazine or membership subscriptions
- Control loyalty and reward schemes
- Prioritise outbound telephone call lists by warmth of the prospect
- Generate sales from existing customers
- Run automated e-mail messages to Web enquirers and buyers
- Automate fulfilment of enquirer packs

## Technological rate of development

The rate of change for computing technology is fast. Very fast. Hardware and software systems, which are used to run marketing databases, are developing in speed and functionality. It is becoming possible to store, process and access customer data in larger and larger volumes and at faster and faster speeds.

Due to computing development, a fully-functioning marketing database is within the reach of even small or cash-poor organisations. A marketing database system can be yours for the price of a software package and a personal computer (PC).

Complex businesses with millions of customers must have an equally sophisticated marketing database.

## Not just a pretty system

Ask the IT experts about what comprises a marketing database and they will invariably say 'hardware' and 'software'. Hardware is the physical computer kit that the system runs on. Software is the programming code that controls the way the system operates and allows your database application to work.

The IT experts are right, yet there is another vital element without which the hardware and software will go to waste: the data.

Data is vital to the effective running of a marketing database system. If you place as much emphasis on data generation, management and use as you do on computer kit, you will be rewarded.

## Structured or relational

There are two main software design types for databases:

1 Structured
2 Relational

Structured databases have a prescribed format into which the data fits. Examples are flat files and hierarchical files. In a flat file, data is held in a series of packages in a long line or string. Hierarchical files are structured much like a family tree with data branches for each family linked to their parents. Again the structure is rigid. Structured databases are effective where data is simple and fairly static, where reporting requirements are unlikely to change and where cost of development is critical.

Relational databases, on the other hand, are flexible. Data need only be input once and is stored in tables linked by ID numbers. The customer ID number is known as the URN or unique reference number. Relational databases can access data to report on any combination of variables with great flexibility. A database set up in Microsoft Access is a relational database.

If data is complex, changes rapidly and requirements cannot be entirely predicted, a relational database works well. The majority of marketing databases are relational.

Organisations implement their marketing databases in different ways, from a single PC to an enterprise-wide system.

## Popular software

There are many software suppliers, ranging from Siebel and Peoplesoft to small-scale databases written in Microsoft Access. Popular systems include: Goldmine, Maximiser, Customer Focus, Mailbrain, ACT! and Outlook. For small companies, shareware is another option. Database shareware can be downloaded from the Web for a minimal registration cost. Additional functionality can be provided through specialist software. Products exist for address management, mail sorting, mass customisation of e-mails and data validation and de-duplication of information.

## What makes a good database?

- Flexible data storage, management, reporting and selection
- Customer-centric view with complete contact and purchase histories for individuals, including campaigns and responses
- Fast performance for search enquiries, input, data loads, selections and reports
- Validation of records, address management and de-duplication of information
- Capable of supporting personalised direct marketing communications, whether website registrations and broadcast emails, telemarketing, direct mail and mobile SMS text messaging
- Tools for analysis and testing, including profiling, scoring, segmentation, tests versus control group

## Creating a marketing database

It can be simple to set up a database. Then again, it can be the most complex and demanding project that you have ever been called upon to complete. The degree of difficulty depends on the complexity of the system, the expertise at your disposal, the level of integration with other systems and the number and diversity of the users.

Perhaps that is why, having analysed numerous database projects that succeeded or failed, Arthur Hughes, the American database expert, advocates:

- Think small and fast – implement within a year at maximum
- Keep an eye on the bottom line – calculate return on investment upfront and aim for that defined outcome

- Use a multi-skilled team with a strong leader
- View requirements from the customers' perspective

*Source: Journal of Database Marketing Vol 5, 1998*

## Successful database projects

To be successful requires strong project management skills and a good mix of technical IT and direct marketing expertise.

*Step 1 Project set up*

- Appoint a project manager and cross-functional team – the team will develop and implement the project, monitoring progress and taking steps to keep it on track
- Develop a detailed project plan showing all the tasks involved plus responsibilities, interim deadlines and critical path
- Agree the budget for the project – set up and ongoing costs
- Set an implementation deadline and agree targets for return on investment with the Board before proceeding further.

*Step 2 Requirements gathering*

- Communicate with users, direct marketers and IT staff so they are aware of the project and know how to provide input
- Conduct a data audit to understand data sources, quality, volumes and processing requirements
- Compile a business requirements specification, detailing the needs that the database system must satisfy

*Step 3 System development*

- Decide to build the database in-house or outsource
- If outsourced, put the work out to tender, obtain proposals and references from three short-listed suppliers – agree contracts with the preferred partner
- Clarify ongoing support required for the project
- Obtain a functional specification from your IT developers to confirm the technical specification for the system
- The developers will design the system and build it

*Step 4 Testing and deploying*

- Provide dummy data for the system developers
- Conduct user acceptance testing to ensure the system works
- Load current data, mapping input files to the new fields
- Consider parallel running of the old and new system during the transition period
- Consider phasing in the adoption of the system by user group
- Conduct user-training, provide a user manual and help desk
- Roll out the complete system; endorse it with a communications programme to explain the benefits to users

*Step 5 Ongoing management*

- Begin ongoing data management activities to keep data accurate and up to date

- Administer access levels, security safeguards and backups
- Utilise the system for strategic planning and campaigns
- Undertake a formal review of the system and take action to achieve financial targets

## Data – the vital ingredient

In order to have accurate and up-to-date information, you must actively manage your data. There is nothing worse than receiving a prospecting call from a company when you have been their customer for the last year. Multiple mailings to the same person waste money and lack credibility. Misspelt names and addresses are irritating and make for poor relationships.

Like the conductor of a great orchestra, the direct marketer must create database music from diverse data sources and data uses.

## Data sources

Data sources will vary depending on your business but could include:

- Telephone enquiries
- Applications
- Web registrations
- Loyalty scheme data
- External lists
- Member-get-member referrals

- Responses to campaigns
- Exhibition enquiries
- Coupon redemptions
- Sales transaction records

## Don't I know you?

Typically, a consumer database will hold information on name, address and contact details, demographics, lifestyle, purchase and promotional history, suppression status and segment. Business data is similar but has the added complication of:

- Parent and subsidiary company relationships
- Different company names within the same group
- Groups of individuals who make buying decisions, including the ultimate decision maker, influencer, gatekeeper and buyer

## Data decay

Remember that your perfect customer or prospect data will not remain accurate without continual refreshment.

| **Consumer markets** 6% of people move house each year | **Business markets** 35% of business data decays in a year |
|---|---|

## Data gremlins

Try to avoid these data gremlins which beset so many databases:

- Out-of-date information used to classify whether the individual has made an enquiry or purchased
- Duplicate customer records
- Poor quality addresses
- Customer name fields containing comments about the person's attitude or likelihood of buying
- Failure to suppress people who have asked not to be contacted

## Data guardians

Your data is more likely to be accurate if you have guardians to look after it:

- Adopt a data culture where everyone who handles data actively helps to ensure it is accurate
- Have system rules governing the completeness and quality of new data, including mandatory input fields and selections from drop-down boxes

- Have strict criteria for the quality of data you buy in from cold lists and rigorously check compliance
- Use the Postcode Address File (PAF), available from the Royal Mail on CD, to validate any of the UK's 27 million addresses and correct poor-quality addresses
- Have systems to accurately de-duplicate customer and enquirer records through merge-purge programmes
- Ensure that you have a complete contact and response history for individual customers
- Suppress people who do not want to be contacted from your direct marketing communications

There are several external files that can be used to clean your data. Clean and accurate data reduces wastage and improves your response and conversion rates.

| Data cleaning | External file |
|---|---|
| Addresses | Postcode address file (PAF) or address management software |
| Deceased | Mortality file, e.g. Smee & Ford, Bereavement Register |
| Movers | Electoral Roll confirms name and address Royal Mail National Change of Address File (NCOA) for redirections; REaD Goneaways File for non-delivered mail |
| No interest | Mailing preference service, telephone preference service, fax preference service and the e-mail preference service |
| Credit risk | Experian and Equifax credit scoring |
| Business change | Companies House data on changes to businesses |

## Summary

Developing and using your marketing database is an important strategic concern. The database is the powerhouse of direct marketing. Hardware, software and data are the key components.

Rapid technological advances continue to open doors for direct marketers, increasing what it is possible to achieve while decreasing costs. Relational marketing databases are very common and offer great flexibility, but structured databases can be appropriate for straightforward applications. Typically, marketing databases are either part of an enterprise-wide CRM system, operate as a stand-alone system taking data feeds from back-office functions or are provided as simple PC-based systems.

Setting up a marketing database from scratch requires a clear vision of how the database will support your business, a precise statement of requirements and an upfront payback model. Strong project management skills are also necessary to make it happen.

Data management is a vital function to ensure an effective marketing database, not least because of the rate of data decay. Avoid data gremlins, such as duplicate records and rely on data guardians to safeguard the integrity of your information. Suppression files are readily available and can save you embarrassment, time and money.

# Selecting the right media

You know your marketplace. You have analysed how the market divides into different customer groups or segments. You have selected the customers and prospects that you will target with a distinctive offer that sets you apart from the competition. Your database is in good shape to support your activity and to allow an ongoing dialogue with prospects and customers. Now it is time to get to grips with the media choices available to you.

## How direct marketers spend their money

Media is the name given to the communications channels available to you, from TV to telemarketing. Spend on direct marketing media has more than trebled since the DMA first began its census in 1994, from £4.1 billion to £11 billion today.

The most used media, ranked in order of importance are:

1  Telemarketing
2  Direct mail
3  TV
4  Door to door
5  Inserts
6  Field marketing
7  National press advertising
8  New media
9  Magazine display
10  Contract magazines
11  Radio
12  Regional display advertising

**13** Outdoor/transport

**14** Cinema

*Source: The DMA Research Centre 2002 Advertising Association.*

Telemarketing is currently the leading direct marketing medium by spend. Spend on direct mail continues to increase, despite the advent of new media and the use of TV as a direct-response medium. The database takes a pivotal role in communications and it is an important budgetary consideration.

## Media evaluation

There are many media choices available to the direct marketer. To make sensible decisions remember to FISH:

- *Fit*: which media fits your target profile?
- *Influence*: is it the right media to influence what target customers think, feel and do in order to get a response?
- *Scale*: can you reach enough of your target audience?
- *Hit*: is it the best channel in terms of cost per hit, i.e. cost per coverage, cost per response and cost per sale?

## Budgeting for media

Costs can vary quite widely. This information is provided as
a general guide. Always check the costs when planning
campaigns and watch out for media inflation.

| Guide to costs for direct marketing media | |
| --- | --- |
| **Media** | **Cost per thousand (CPT)** |
| **TV**<br>National and regional direct response TV | £5–10 |
| **National press**<br>Tabloid, for a 25cm × four-column, mono advert<br>Broadsheet, for a 25cm × four column, mono advert | £5<br>£20 |
| **New media**<br>Internet banner advert, cost is per thousand<br>page impressions | £15 |
| **Inserts**<br>In national press/consumer titles, for A5 size,<br>colour printed insert, media cost includes print | £40 |
| **Door-to-door**<br>With targeting by area and neighbourhood type, for<br>an A5 size, colour printed leaflet, cost includes print | £55 |

**Direct mail**
Well targeted direct mail, including printing,      £500
personalisation and enclosing, from 50p per
mail pack

**Telemarketing**
Inbound call handling, from £2 a call      £2,000
Outbound call competition, from £2.50 a call    £2,500

**Field marketing**
Salesperson face-to-face appointment    £50–200 per
appointment

Note: Guide prices exclude VAT and are based upon information from the
Institute of Direct Marketing.

Remember that media costs are one element of campaign
costs. Ensure that, where appropriate, you also budget for:

- Agency fees
- Design, copy, artwork, Web animations, lists and
  print production where not included in media costs
- Response handling, data capture, fulfilment
  materials and incentives
- Freephone, freepost and business reply postage
- Couriers and deliveries
- Insurance, redemption indemnity costs
- Legal fees
- Direct marketing operation overheads

## Response rates by media

The number of potential customers that respond to a
campaign can vary dramatically. Here is a general guide, but
find out the norms for your business. Accurate targeting and

media selection, together with a compelling proposition, will encourage prospects to act and act now.

| Guide to response rates by direct marketing media | | |
|---|---|---|
| **Media** | **Response rate** | **Response volume** |
| Face-to-face calling | 10–30% | 10–30 per 100 appointments |
| Outbound telemarketing | 5–10% | 5–10 per 100 completed calls |
| Direct mail | 1–4% | 1–4 per 100 mailed |
| Door-to-door | 0.2% | 2 per 1,000 households |
| New media banner ads | 0.1–0.5% | 1–5 per 1,000 web surfers viewing ad |
| Loose inserts | 0.1–0.5% | 1–5 per 1,000 readers |
| National press | 0.075% | 7.5 out of 10,000 readers |
| TV | 0.05% | 5 out of 10,000 viewers |

Note: Response rates are provided for guidance only, based upon information from The Institute of Direct Marketing. Response rates vary widely depending on the product, targeting, offer, timing, creative treatment and response mechanism.

Remember that cost management and media selection must go hand in hand.

## Pros and cons by media

Which media should you use within your direct marketing campaigns? The answer depends on who you are targeting and what you want them to think, feel and do. Let's take each of the core media in turn.

*Outbound telemarketing*

| Plus | Minus |
|------|-------|
| • Personalised and can readily pre-qualify contacts (call first to identify the right person) | • Expensive cost/contact |
| | • Difficult to contact certain people: 5 per cent households without phones, ex-directory numbers, business numbers using voicemail, mobiles |
| • Infinitely testable | |
| • Quick to deploy | |
| | • Lacks visual stimulus |
| | • Can be viewed as intrusive |

Good for generating business appointments, converting enquirers, persuading waiverers and taking orders.

*Direct mail*

| Plus | Minus |
|------|-------|
| • Personalised and infinitely targetable and controllable | • More costly than door drops |
| • Less expensive than tele-marketing and face-to-face | • Requires data management skills |
| • Can convey detailed and complex information | • Can be high wastage due to small percentage response |
| • Can include reply-paid cards, vouchers and pre-completed forms | • Data errors in name and address production lack professionalism |

Widely used where individual records of customers and prospects are available on the database or via external lists.

*TV*

| Plus | Minus |
|------|-------|
| • Excellent for creating awareness, influencing hearts and minds and building brands | • Not personalised |
| | • Can only convey a small amount of information |
| • Great for reaching large audiences | • Expensive production costs |
| | • Needs memorable phone number and Web address |
| • Good where hand raising is required | • Limited ability to target |
| • Can work for niche markets where programming matches targeting | • Increasingly fragmented audiences not reflected in advertising cost reductions |

Used where a mass audience exists, where niche audiences match target profile, and where self-identification is required.

*Door-to-door*

| Plus | Minus |
|------|-------|
| • Far cheaper than direct mail for mass markets | • Can only target by household, not by person |
| • Can select by household, e.g. within a store catchment area | • High wastage due to low % response |
| • Can provide trial samples | • Can aggravate customers if prospects are offered a better deal |

Used for mass markets; small businesses can target precisely, by walking from house-to-house, door-dropping certain households e.g. driveways needing repair.

*Loose inserts*

| Plus | Minus |
|------|-------|
| • Greater scope than press ad for use of colour, different formats, different printing techniques, e.g. scratchcard and use of regional tests<br>• Good for postal responses, e.g. used for photo film envelopes | • Not personalised, less control over who reads insert<br>• More expensive than press ads<br>• Insert can be lost or messages diluted amongst other companies' inserts |

Widely used where target profile and readership profile match. Higher costs of inserts versus press ads can be offset by increased response.

*Face-to-face calling*

| Plus | Minus |
|------|-------|
| • Primary media for high cost business-to-business and consumer purchases<br>• Can build rapport with multiple decision makers<br>• Allows a two-way dialogue and the opportunity to overcome objections by providing more information | • Very expensive compared to other media<br>• Needs phone and database support to work well<br>• Cannot reach mass audiences this way<br>• Requires skilled salespeople |

Used for high cost sales. Normally an essential part of the business-to-business media mix.

*National press*

| Plus | Minus |
|------|-------|
| • Cost-effective media where offering has broad appeal | • Not personalised |
| • Can create an impact and be persuasive | • High fixed cost per ad, run risk of low response levels |
| • Allows more scope for testing than TV | • Best times to advertise are also best times for competitors to advertise – message can be diluted alongside competitor ads |
| • Can use advertorials – ad and editorial combined | |
| • Unlike TV, can also offer postal response route | • Not good for narrow or local market segments |

Used where a mass audience exists, used for one-stage and two-stage sales, heavily used for financial services.

*Web banner ads*

| Plus | Minus |
|------|-------|
| • Low production costs | • Certain sections of society do not have Web access |
| • Can use free banner ad exchange schemes or negotiate charges per click through | • Click throughs may not result in sales |
| | • Banner ads are relatively expensive versus press |
| • Get more than a response, link to website with data collection and online ordering | • Your success is reliant on the ability of the supplier to drive traffic to their site and your website to convert visits into sales |
| • It is discreet for sensitive services | |

Used by a broad range of companies to reach target audiences and drive traffic to their websites. Flexible and quick to deploy.

## Other media choices

The media that we have focused upon is where most of the money gets spent, but it is not the complete picture. Think about the appropriate way to reach your target market. Be open minded and also consider:

- *Magazine display*: similar advantages to press, but allows more refined targeting.
- *Outdoor/transport*: can target by journeys and traveller type.
- *Radio*: similar to TV, opportunities for sponsorship and competitions as well as response advertising.
- *Regional press*: useful for local services
- *Contract magazines*: important for many companies, including the AA and Saga.
- *Cinema*: used for local services and targeted campaigns. Can align age of target audience with film certificate ratings.
- *Website*: excellent vehicle for interaction with potential customers, can capture detailed information and take online orders.
- *E-mail*: low cost compared to direct mail because no print or postage. Can include links to campaign landing-pages and websites.
- *SMS mobile text messaging*: can convey simple messages. Provides immediate response mechanism.
- *Exhibitions*: often used for generating leads for business-to-business products and services, also used for certain consumer audiences, e.g. weddings, crafts, home décor.
- *On-pack*: used in conjunction with promotions to attract trialists and gain data on existing customers.
- *In-pack*: allows collection of data on customers, used for consumer goods, can also include money-off vouchers and collect-and-claim offers.

- *In-store point of sale*: for collection of data on customers and competitor customers, especially used for consumer goods.

## Media medley

Reaching the right customers entails selecting the most appropriate and cost-effective media. It is important to appreciate that many media can work together. As a direct marketer, you need to be able to blend different media for maximum impact.

Consider the case of a new consumer utilities provider. At launch the business uses broad-scale advertising to generate awareness and responses for customer acquisition. DRTV and national press will form the media platform. The contact centre will handle phone and website responses. Fulfilment will be carried out by e-mail and direct mail.

As the customer base grows, the business will focus on customer retention and cross-sell opportunities via direct mail and e-mail. It will use telemarketing and internet banner advertising to top up the customer bank by acquiring new customers from the potential switchers in the market.

## Media know-how

Make good use of the resources at your disposal to help you with media selection and targeting:

- Media packs provide audience profiles and statistics
- Expertise of consultants and media planners
- Competitor media behaviour and claimed successes
- Your company's past campaign performance

## Summary

Getting to grips with media involves an understanding of broad-scale and personalised media choices. Media selection requires you to FISH. This means assessing the Fit with your target market, the Influence that media can make, the Scale of coverage required and the cost per Hit. Cost management and media selection are two sides of the same coin.

In practice, most direct marketers blend a variety of different media in order to achieve their objectives. You must do this to maximise the overall response, playing to the strengths of each media to exploit its full potential.

# Creating and executing campaigns

The creation and delivery of direct marketing campaigns may be one of the most stimulating roles that you are called upon to perform. There is something for everyone because this job requires the skills of the:

- Analyst
- Producer
- Psychologist
- Entrepreneur
- Logistics manager
- Wordsmith
- Artist
- Lawyer

## Why does my company need a campaign?

Direct marketing campaigns bring your choice of strategic direction alive through operational plans which allow you to reach your destination.

Your organisation may run a single direct marketing campaign during the year, or a multitude of campaigns at different times, focusing on different products and services. Whichever it is, campaigns are about tangible actions and delivery of results.

## Campaign development

All that you have learned and achieved so far is of value when drawing up a campaign plan. You know where you are now. You have already decided where you want to be and you have set objectives. The strategic direction you plan to take has also been mapped out. Now you need to make it happen. For each strategy you need to set out a series of actions.

The good news is that you have already tackled three important areas which will form part of your plan:

- Segmentation and targeting
- The marketing database
- Media selection

## Allowable marketing costs

Before you become absorbed in elaborate plans or entrepreneurial deals, you need to be sure of your budget. Set an allowable marketing cost to decide an acceptable and appropriate direct marketing budget to get the company to its destination and achieve the required sales or profit level.

Take the sales targets you set for direct marketing activity.
Then, based on the required level of return on investment
(ROI), calculate acceptable direct marketing costs. For example:

| | |
|---|---|
| Sales target | £1,000,000 |
| ROI | 20:1, i.e. spend £1, get £20 in sales revenue |
| Budget | £1,000,000 ÷ 20 = |
| | £50,000 allowable direct marketing spend |

You must also decide how to split the budget between:

- Acquisition campaigns or retention campaigns
- Building your database or managing and using your data
- Use of broad-scale or personalised media
- Generating responses or converting responses into sales

Having established your budget, you must get creative to
gain maximum punch for every direct marketing pound.

## What product and service are you offering?

Consider product features and benefits, price and what
differentiates the product from competitor products. Will
you develop the product, replace it, enhance it, customise it
or change delivery, maintenance or payment options?

## Do you need any research and database analysis?

You have learned a great deal by analysing your customers,
capability and competitors and by completing a SWOT

analysis. Are there any gaps in your knowledge? Decide whether you will obtain information by further database analysis, by analysing published research or by commissioning new research.

## Which markets and segments will you compete in?

Your strategy will explain which markets and segments you will operate in at a broad level. Now add some detail. Define each segment, its size, profile and value.

## What is your proposition?

Your product or service has many features; it is used in different ways and offers different benefits. You need to provide a compelling reason for customers to choose you and to stay loyal. Is it the same proposition for all segments or is it different? Will you use added offers or incentives?

| | |
|---|---|
| Why should I choose you? | Answer this and you have an overall proposition. |
| What's the big deal here? | Answer this and you have an offer. |

## How will you find and acquire new customers?

What is your specific target profile for new customers? Where will you find new customers? Will you use cold lists, advertise in the press or ask existing customers to introduce a friend?

## How will you retain existing customers and sell more?

Which customers will you focus your efforts on? What reinforcement and incentives will you provide to motivate them to stay loyal? Will you offer preferential rates, special recognition, membership rewards, collect-and-claim schemes, points programmes or added-value services?

## How will you build and use your database?

Does your database have enough records already or do you need to find mechanisms to collect customer and prospect data? Will you profile and clone your data to identify lookalike prospects from external lists? What selections will you make for acquisition and retention campaigns? What mail, phone or e-mail lists will you need to trigger automatically, such as renewals due, subscriptions overdue or appointment follow up? What reports and campaign evaluation will you require?

## What about targeting and media selection?

Your acquisition and retention campaigns must specify your target prospect profile and target customer profile by segment. Who exactly will you select and who will you avoid? Which specific media will you use to attract new customers? Which specific media will you use to keep existing customers? How many people can you reach by each of the selected media? What format will your message take, for example, advert position and size, contents of mail pack, length and structure of outbound phone call? How many responses and sales do you forecast?

## What tests will you run?

Testing is covered on Saturday in greater detail. For now, consider what you need to test. Remember the campaign factors listed in priority order on page 34. Here are the figures showing the impact these factors can have upon performance.

*Difference between best and worst performance by factor*

| Factor | Impact on response |
|--------|--------------------|
| Targeting | × 6 |
| Offer | × 3 |
| Timing | × 2 |
| Creative and format | × 1.35 |
| Response mechanism | × 1.2 |

Remember that, after your product or service, the most important thing to test is targeting.

## What about timing?

When will you run the campaign? Do you want to create a big impact in a short space of time or can you spread activity throughout the year? Is there a good time for people to act? Consider timing at a top level and in detail – seasonality, peaks and troughs, contract renewal cycle, company budget year and accounting year end, annual renewals month and date, birth date and age triggers, day of the week, time of day and stated preference for best time to call.

## Which creative treatment will provoke a response?

You know the product or service that you are promoting.

You have decided on the proposition that makes your product distinct from the competition and provides a compelling reason for your target audience to take action. How will you explain what you have to offer in words and pictures (and sounds if you are using the phone, radio, TV or the internet)?

What hooks can you use to gain interest and what likely objections must you overcome?

| Hooks | Objections |
|---|---|
| Save money | Too cheap |
| Make money | Too expensive |
| Quick and easy | Takes too long |
| Reliable and fewer problems | Don't want it |
| Feel good | Don't know you |
| More prestigious | Don't like you |
| Well-known brand | Don't believe you |

Build a mental picture of the people you are targeting. Think in their language. For example, is a savings product 'extra cash' or 'an intelligent investment'?

Determine how you will adapt the overall campaign theme to maximise the response potential of each media and play to the strengths that each media has in the communications mix.

## What response mechanism and call to action is appropriate?

All direct marketing communications must include a call to action. Having conveyed your selling message, you need to let potential customers know what you want them to do next.

Your call to action might be one of the following:

- 'Call free on 0800 123 456 for an immediate quote'
- 'Just clip the coupon for 50p off your next purchase'
- 'Fax back to request an engineer's appointment'
- 'Click here for even more savings'
- 'Sign the pre-approved form and return, postage free'

Freephone and freepost response options tend to uplift response.

Broadcast media relies on memorable phone numbers or website addresses. Business communications often use Web links and fax-backs, as well as phone lines. Direct mail can include a phone number, voucher, website address and a personalised postal coupon or application.

The secret is to match the preferences of your customers. Provide the response mechanisms that work best for each media. Give incentives for responding. Test the impact that offering a 'choice' of response channel has on uplifting overall response.

## Convert responses into sales

When developing your campaign, consider how you will apportion your budget between generating responses and converting those responses into sales. Too many organisations fail to put enough thought into how they will convert responses into sales. Do not be one of them.

Consider how to maximise the value of each response with:

- Immediate and professional handling of inbound phone calls, faxes, e-mails and applications
- Campaign landing pages within your website with easy navigation for placing orders
- Communications that reinforce the original proposition and provide incentives to act now

This applies whether your company has a one- or two-stage sales process. One-stage is where the customer places an order in response to your direct marketing. Two-stage is where you generate initial enquiries that then become sales. At every stage you require a strong call to action clearly stating what customers should do next and providing reasons to act now.

To close the sale you can use:

- Deadlines for applications
- Reminders
- Bonuses and preferential rates for early responses
- Money-back guarantee if not satisfied
- Extra incentives, such as initial month free, free warranty

## Keep it legal

Direct marketers need to be mindful of the laws that govern their business. Complying with the law is not optional – you must make sure that you operate within the law or you will face the consequences.

Codes of practice exist to provide helpful guidance on required standards:

- The Direct Marketing Authority Code of Practice
- The British Codes for Advertising and Sales Promotions

## Data protection fundamentals

Compliance with the Data Protection Act (DPA) is fundamental for direct marketers. The Act states that personal data must be fairly and lawfully obtained, used for the purpose it was given, securely processed and that explicit permission must be sought for collection of sensitive data. Safeguards are also required where data is transferred to non-EU countries. Make sure that you comply. For example:

- Are you registered under the DPA?
- Does your direct mail and e-mail allow recipients to opt out?
- Do your inbound phone calls ask for permission to retain information for marketing purposes?
- Does your website have an unmissable privacy policy?
- Do you ask for permission to collect 'sensitive' data, such as race, religion and health?

Guidance can be obtained from the Information Commissioner for Data Protection.

Remember, while codes of practice provide valuable guidance, there is no substitute for professional legal advice. Ensure that your company lawyer is involved in your plans and formally approves your direct marketing adverts, scripts and materials.

## Summary

Direct marketing campaigns bring your strategy to life, delivering the results you require. Make certain that you set a sensible budget and have specific actions for:

- Your product or service
- Extra research or analysis
- Segmentation
- Your proposition
- Acquisition of new customers
- Retention of existing customers
- The database
- Targeting and media
- Testing
- Creative treatment
- Generating responses
- Converting responses into sales

With detailed schedules for developing the campaign and planned timings for all activities and communications, you remain in control.

# Measurement and management of success

By now you will be familiar with the features of direct marketing. You know that:

- An understanding of customers is based upon individual data
- All communication is designed to get a response
- Interaction and personalisation is facilitated by a marketing database
- Strategies are based on both customer acquisition and, importantly, on customer retention
- Every aspect of a direct marketing campaign can be tested
- Results can be accurately measured

The latter two aspects of testing and measurement are explored in more detail today.

## The three Rs – record, review and refine

The beauty of direct marketing is that it is accountable. When you have sound strategies and campaigns that hit the mark, your achievements are clear for all to see. Even better, you do not have to gamble your entire budget on one course of action.

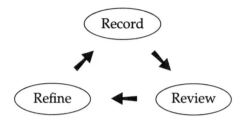

You can build a successful direct marketing platform by testing different options and backing those that work best. Then you can strive to beat the top performing campaigns.

Results are recorded, reviewed and refined in a circle of continuous improvement. Let's look at each of the three Rs in turn.

## Recording individual data

With accurate information to draw upon, you are in control. You can use the data to ensure you reach your direct marketing destination.

*Get the basics right*
Ensure you use separate fields to record each element of a person's name and address, including their postcode. Unless address variables are separated, you will be hampered when you want to verify them and de-duplicate or personalise communications.

*Record results at an individual level*
Log responses and sales by individual person. You can measure not just the overall campaign, but drill down for further insights.

*Track data sources*
Make sure that you know where new data originates from.
Give source codes to your own data, bought-in lists and
general enquiries. This way you can track the best
performing data sources.

*Note the campaign code*
Use campaign codes as a shorthand to describe when the
campaign ran, who was targeted, what media was used and
which test was used.

Make sure campaign codes are accurately recorded when
responses are received. For example, by printing them on
press response coupons, asking inbound callers and making
campaign codes a mandatory part of data input.

*Record the financial as well as the physical*
Make life easy for yourself. Keep accurate records of the
actual campaign costs for all activities, broken down into sub-
campaigns and test cells. Many companies keep strict records
of the number of responses and sales, but fail to apply
standards to the way they calculate and apportion costs. It can
be very difficult to backtrack and review historic performance
if you do not keep a precise log of costs as you go along.

## Reviewing and measuring results

There is an old business saying: 'What gets measured gets
done'. There are certain standard measures that are useful
when reviewing results – make good use of them.

*Overall measures of success*
Senior management's interest in direct marketing is top line:
'Did we hit forecast, on time and within budget?'

Key measures are:

- Return on Investment (ROI) – profit/spend and sales/spend
- Sales turnover – total sales revenue
- Profit contribution – sales less costs (goods sold, distribution and direct marketing)
- Market share – % sales, by volume or value

*Tools in the box*
The direct marketer has a raft of additional, useful measures which include:

- Standard campaign measures
- Customer measures
- Database measures
- Media measures

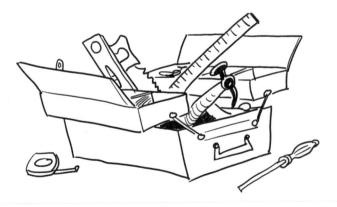

*Standard campaign measures*

| | |
|---|---|
| Response rate | = (number of responses/ audience) × 100 |
| Cost per response (CPR) | = cost/number responses |
| Conversion rate | = (number of sales/number of responses) × 100 |
| Cost per sale (CPS) | = cost/number of sales |
| Average order value (AOV) | = value of sales/number of sales |

Take a campaign:

| | |
|---|---|
| Costs | £10,000 |
| Audience | 20,000 |
| Number of responses | 1000 |
| Number of sales | 250 |
| Sales value | £50,000 |

The campaign results are:

| | |
|---|---|
| Response rate | 5% |
| Cost per response | £10 |
| Conversion rate | 25% |
| Cost per sale | £40 |
| Average order value | £200 |

*Customer measures*

As well as measuring campaign responses, measure results at a customer level.

- Volume of prospects and customers acquired
- Customer base growth rate, i.e. % volume increase
- Customer repeat purchase rate, i.e. % cross-sales

- Attrition rate, i.e. % customers lost per annum
- Retention rate, i.e. % customers kept per annum

Remember to use the measures of customer value which were covered at the outset:

- Pareto 80:20 customer value
- Recency, frequency and monetary value
- Customer lifetime value

*Monitor timing*

Response tracking and forecasting is essential when you have an in-house contact centre, sales team or fulfilment team. Measure responses over time by media and use this for staffpower planning and stock management.

If you know that 100 per cent of the responses to a campaign are received within three months, but 80 per cent are received in a week, you do not have to wait long to know if your campaign will be a success. After just one week, you will have a very clear idea.

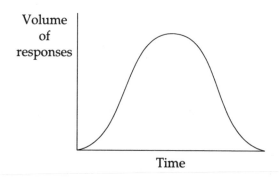

**Response curve**

Monitor the impact of other timing measures to maximise your effectiveness. For instance, work out the ideal timing to issue advance renewal notices and reminders. Some companies have found that older customers like to make buying decisions well before the renewal deadline, while younger ones will respond up to the final whistle.

*Specific media measures*
The standard campaign measures are widely used across all media. In addition, there are some terms peculiar to the media they are measuring.

*Telemarketing*

- Calls answered – the % of calls answered
- Calls abandoned – the % of calls received where the caller hangs up before they get put through
- Average time to answer – waiting time in seconds
- Call duration – average length of call
- % of calls completed – outbound calls where the contact person was available and the call was completed
- % supervised transfers – % of calls where the caller had to be referred to a second tier of support in order to answer their query

*Direct mail*

- % of goneaways – percentage of packs that could not be delivered
- % of response by mailing cell

*Direct response TV*

- Opportunities to see (OTS) is used to measure the actual audience achieved during a TV campaign compared to forecasts
- Responses are measured by creative treatment and per channel or station, per daypart, per position within the commercial break, by frequency shown and by length of commercial

*Database*

- Total customer and prospect records
- Recency of records – when last updated
- Field occupancy rates – % of records where data is complete
- Rate of data decay – % of data on the database that becomes out of date within a year
- % opt out – number of customer records where you must not make further marketing contact

*National press advertising*

- OTS is used to measure the average number of times a reader will see an advert
- Response as a % of circulation and also by position
- Share of voice – percentage of ad spend versus competitors

*Inserts*

- Response per distribution type – solus, shared
- Response per insert type – loose, bound-in, tipped-on (glued), in-pack

*Door-to-door*

- Response as a % of households targeted
- % penetration of targets by postcode – showing percentage of targets that will be hit by selecting specific postcodes

*Field marketing*

- Hot, warm and cold sales leads
- Number of appointments, proposals, tenders
- Cost per appointment

*Web*

- Site visit – customer visit to a website
- Average length of visit – time spent viewing and interacting with your website

- Referring site – which other site has the visitor clicked on to reach your website, i.e. the source of your website traffic?
- Page impressions – number of times the page has been viewed
- Registrations – number of visitors supplying data
- Average basket value – average spend per customer per visit

*Add research for greater insights*
Direct marketing measures explain what has happened, research can explain why. Use it to supplement your understanding of:

- The reasons why people did or did not buy
- Attitudes to your company, products and services in comparison to the competition
- Customer satisfaction and commitment to your company

## Refining for continuous improvement

To be a good direct marketer you need to do two things:

1 Pre-empt the results that you might get by planning for contingencies
2 Embrace the need to continually beat your results – use a cycle of testing and roll out of improvements

*Contingency planning*
Be ready for the unexpected:

- Constantly monitor results versus forecast during each campaign
- Set aside part of your direct marketing budget to allow room for manoeuvre if results do not turn out as expected
- Plan for contingencies, such as responses being higher or lower than target
- Decide what steps you will take if you need to improve conversion rates or increase average order values

*Testing, testing, 1, 2, 3 . . .*

It is vital to construct robust tests, measure their relative performance and incorporate the learning into future campaigns. Not only does it move your organisation forward, it is also very rewarding.

*How do you go about testing?*

- Establish your current best direct marketing performer by media. This is your 'Control'.
- Decide how much budget to put into your previously tried and tested campaigns and how much into your tests in order to find new campaigns.
- Try to beat the control. Remember to test the most critical factors first and set SMART performance targets. After your product or service, the factors to test are:
  - Targeting
  - Offer
  - Timing
  - Creative and format
  - Response mechanism

- Assess roll-out potential of each test to help you decide where to focus your efforts.
- Although creative is a lower priority, changing the creative treatment and format can have a significant impact where there is little room to further improve the targeting, offer or timing.
- Make sure that you only test one variable at a time. If you change more than one thing, you will not know with any certainty which factor produced the change in results. Construct a test matrix to control this process.
- Take care to make sure that the results you get are statistically significant and inspire confidence. Achieving 20 responses instead of ten is a 50 per cent uplift, but do you really want to base future plans on the behaviour of just 20 respondents?

Refer to your company accountant, statistician or planner. Your organisation may even have a look-up table that sets out the volumes required for certain tests. If you do not have any of these, find out what scale of results will allow you and your senior managers to make decisions and agree this prior to testing.

*Test matrix*
This example shows a test matrix for a direct mail campaign, where list sources and creative treatment are tested.

| Test cell | List | Creative | Test quantity | Roll-out quantity |
|---|---|---|---|---|
| 1 | A – Control list | Control pack | 10,000 | 50,000 |
| 2 | A – Control list | New pack | 10,000 | 50,000 |
| 3 | B | Control pack | 10,000 | 40,000 |
| 4 | C | Control pack | 10,000 | 70,000 |

Cell 1 uses the best performing list and mail pack. It is our control. To assess performance of the lists, compare the alternative test cells 3 and 4 with cell 1. To assess the performance of the creative, compare the new pack in cell 2 to cell 1. As you can see, the test matrix allows us to test different factors while only altering one variable at a time.

*Propensity to respond or buy*
Employ the information you have gained from running campaigns and develop a scoring model of respondents and buyers. Identify the attributes that are predictive of success. Utilise this information to select the most responsive targets and to avoid those unlikely to respond. This will increase the cost-efficiency of your activity.

*Sanity check your segmentation*
Analyse the groups of prospects and customers on your database. Use this knowledge to guide future activity.

Have any of these individuals moved from one segment to another? For example, have any lapsed customers been reactivated? If so, what campaigns are now appropriate for them?

Does the information gleaned from campaigns support your segmentation of the market or does your segmentation now need revision? For instance, if you have one segment which now accounts for 50 per cent of your records, it could be further sub-divided to ensure that activity remains relevant to individual customers and prospects. Again, statistical modelling techniques can help to develop a meaningful customer segmentation.

## Summary

Recording and reviewing results enables you to refine your direct marketing strategy and campaigns. Use the raft of measurement tools to evaluate your strategy. Refine activity by contingency planning and by running tests, which can be rolled out as part of a continuous improvement cycle.

The three Rs are a feature of direct marketing. They lead to greater success, greater profit and greater recognition for you.

## Direct marketing round-up

Lord Leverhulme is famously reported as saying:

> *'Half the money I spend on advertising is wasted, the trouble is I don't know which half.'*

He was not a direct marketer or he would have been able to account for every penny.

By being creative, in the broad sense of the word, you can maximise the punch for your pound. You will know precisely what impact your expenditure has made upon customer lifetime values, turnover and profit.

Technology will continue to be an enabling factor for acquisition and retention strategies. New messaging innovations will provide alternative media channels for direct communications. The rapid uptake in internet usage presents increasing scope for the direct marketer to interact with prospects and customers in a responsive environment.

With direct marketing you can give your customers what they want and enjoy commercial success.

## The next stage

Dee Twomey runs Marketing Zone, a marketing communications company that specialises in developing direct marketing programmes.

Further information can be obtained from:

- Marketing Zone: 01763 274440
- dee@marketingzone.co.uk
- www.marketingzone.co.uk

Enjoy being direct!

SUN

MON

TUE

WED

THU

FRI

SAT

For information

on other

**IN A** **WEEK** titles

go to

www.inaweek.co.uk